Rescue Me

Forerunners: Ideas First

Short books of thought-in-process scholarship, where intense analysis, questioning, and speculation take the lead

FROM THE UNIVERSITY OF MINNESOTA PRESS

(Continued on page 70)

Rescue Me
On Dogs and Their Humans

Margret Grebowicz

University of Minnesota Press

MINNEAPOLIS
LONDON

Portions of this book were previously published in Margret Grebowicz, "You Are Not the Boss of Your Dog," *Slate,* September 21, 2021, https://slate.com/technology/2021/09/cesar-millan-dominance -theory-dog-training.html, and in Margret Grebowicz, "In Defense of the Dog Bowl," *The Philosophical Salon,* January 27, 2020, https://thephilosophicalsalon.com/in-defense-of-the-dog-bowl/.

ISBN 978-1-5179-1460-8 (pb)
ISBN 978-1-4529-6875-9 (Ebook)
ISBN 978-1-4529-6876-6 (Manifold)

Published by the University of Minnesota Press, 2022
111 Third Avenue South, Suite 290
Minneapolis, MN 55401-2520
http://www.upress.umn.edu

Available as a Manifold edition at manifold.umn.edu

The University of Minnesota is an equal-opportunity educator and employer.

Contents

Introduction: Confessions of a Dog Hoarder

I DREAM OF MORE DOGS. When I fantasize about a life of success, my future, much-improved self is surrounded by dogs. Like many dog lovers, I am a fancier of a particular breed: the basenji, also called the African barkless dog. Like a hoarder, I want more. But I could just as well surround myself with chihuahuas. Or I could just devote myself to dogs with special needs or old dogs who need a hospice. The shelters are overflowing with pit bulls, after all, and many people give up large dogs when they get to be too big to handle. Or for no reason except because they are sick. I could be a haven for them, for all of them.

When I imagine my own forever home, it's never the home itself that I see, or even the landscape. Being settled down—finally, once and for all—boils down to exactly one thing: more dogs. Financial stability = more dogs. Structure and routine = dogs. Mental health = dogs. A happy family = dogs. Buoyed by these fantasies, I am no different than a dog hoarder, except that my armies of dogs are in my dreams.

Where does animal hoarding begin? Does it not begin, precisely, with desire? Reading Abigail Thomas's extraordinary memoir *A Three Dog Life* I catch myself envying her that third dog and reveling in her accounts of climbing into bed with her troika, all four of them cuddling deliciously for warmth and comfort, against the rest of the world. And what a world it is: the book is mainly about the tragic accident in which her husband suffers permanent brain damage and must live out the rest of his days in a nursing home. Despite that, I find myself delighting—along with her—in her new, single-human family, and in the preposterous luxury that is that third dog. That's the thing: no one is around to tell her how many dogs she is allowed to adopt, what size they should be, or whether or not they should sleep in the bed. Thomas herself may not be a hoarder, but I am certain that my own pleasure in reading her is mildly inappropriate, as my whole being keeps asking for permission to get just one more.

In real life, I live with two dogs: one basenji (Abba) and one chihuahua (Waffles). So I'm due for a third, right?

When I confess this to friends, they reassure me by explaining that there's a world of difference between fantasizing about something and actually doing it. But, given that animal hoarding is now recognized as a mental illness, I am secretly convinced that its roots are precisely in fantasy, and that I'm pulsating with this inappropriate desire. And clearly, I'm not alone.

In *Confessions: Animal Hoarding,* a documentary-reality TV series that premiered in 2010, an elderly woman lives in filth with more than two hundred cats, her family in despair and alienated. An overweight young gay man with more than thirty chihuahuas, which bark incessantly. Dogs interbreed at will, fill yards with their feces, fight over food. Sick cats live in cages. There's constant noise, punctuated by whispers invoking "diseases." Most of the hoarders unemployed or on the verge of it, their spouses and fiancés threatening divorce, and adult children refusing to bring their kids over to see grandma, who remains incomprehensibly impervious to any intervention.

As grandma calmly explains that her dogs take priority over

seeing her grandchildren, it's clear that she is in pain. The source of that pain is less clear. The family members—and we, the viewers—wring hands over what could possibly have gone wrong with grandma to make her this way. I am both covering my face in horror and peeking out through the spaces between my fingers. Hoarders overwhelmingly tend to be white women, middle aged and older. While on a good day, my imagined life unfolds in a gleaming interspecies paradise, on a bad day what I see in every one of these episodes is my not-so-distant future self.

Were I watching *Confessions* in public, I'd be looking around to see if others felt the same way. Is it just me, or is the depiction of grandma's übernormal family enough to send anyone into hoarding, just to keep those unbearable, judgmental people at bay? Surely, everyone gets why she breaks down sobbing at the very mention of losing any one of her dogs, even when she has eighty-seven of them. And what about that horrible husband who is "grossed out" by having to clean up cat feces? Does anyone actually like him, or do we all agree that auntie is actually much better off single? That husband, just like those children, has no interest in the actual source of the pain she's experiencing— or conversely, in the sense of purpose that she gets—however delusionally—from "saving" animals. Instead, the alleged "loved ones" put constant, unrelenting pressure on their "loved one" to surrender the truly loved ones, the animals, to the town authorities and thus never see them again.

The show posits the hoarder as the source of the problem, not everyone around her, not her past, not her actual poverty or feelings of scarcity and precarity, not her or fear of abandonment. No one seems interested in learning about this citadel she has built—the animals in the show are often described as a "buffer"— and how it functions to keep her feeling safe and sane, buoyed by occasional experiences of love, attention, and abundance— everything she is otherwise lacking and has probably gone without for her whole life. The family "just" wants grandma or mom or auntie or daughter or grandpa or son (when the hoarders are men) "back"—back in the world that the hoarder learned long ago doesn't actually want them at all.

Is this really a show about some antisocial freaks living on the fringes of society and abusing dogs and cats, or is it surreptitiously designed to expose how disappointing and internally destructive every attempt at closeness with humans ultimately becomes? I've come to this show for the former, but the take-home, at least for me, is without a doubt the latter.

It's difficult to say exactly what kind of mental illness animal hoarding is. It was once linked to compulsive disorders but is now increasingly linked to depression, anxiety, and social isolation. In all cases of hoarding, the perpetrators feel a strong need to protect their animals from society. There is even a subcategory called "rescue hoarding," where hoarders are convinced that they are the only people on earth who can help these animals. Furthermore, relapses happen in 100 percent of hoarders when their animals are taken away and no ongoing support is available. Unfortunately, that necessary support is usually the stuff that was in short supply to begin with: empathy, community, patience, therapy for trauma, and long-term, collaborative intervention by multiple agencies, families, and friends.

Who has that these days?

It's easy to condemn animal hoarding because it results in actual victims, the animals. Animals recovered from hoarding situations are famously traumatized, neglected, sometimes starved. Often, they've lived their whole lives in dark rooms or other cramped enclosures, in their own waste, in need of medical attention, and in need of grooming and proper socialization, which they have never received. Such dogs require special skills, patience, and time from potential adopters. They might be neurotic, pathologically shy, or aggressive. They don't know how to live with people. They don't necessarily know how to live with dogs, even though they have lived with dogs their whole lives. They may have disorders resulting from generations of inbreeding. And when hoarders fear giving up their dogs because they might be killed by the state, they're not exactly wrong. If the dog is feral enough, the odds are that it will show aggression and be declared beyond rehabilitation.

If we take the perpetrators to be the hoarders themselves, we are faced with a clear-cut case of animal abuse. But if, just for a moment, we imagine the hoarders as victims, too, the story—and our own place in it—changes dramatically. *Confessions* brings us people who are themselves living in filth, stuck in cycles of trauma and social withdrawal, poor, neglected, ashamed—indeed, shamed into hiding. From this perspective, dog hoarding emerges not as a deplorable practice of the insane but as a symptom of a sick society unable to support its members, both human and nonhuman.

During one of my recent visits to the local SPCA, just to have a look around to see who might be up for adoption, I ended up going home with a hoarded dog I named Maybelline. I told myself that I was not interested in adopting her (though I'm due for a third, let's not forget), but once I heard her story I agreed to foster her for a week. A one-year-old mix of beagle and blue heeler, she was petite, agile, very intelligent, and—as I discovered as the Trazodone wore off—suffering from the worst anxiety I have ever seen. For the first day, she panted incessantly, paced, and destroyed the house in various efforts to escape. By day two, she had run off twice, and once she discovered herself back in the terrifying prison that was my home, she began baying to some unknown someone. She called out for more than twenty-four hours, but no one responded. On day three, the baying suddenly ceased. She had decided that the house was where she wanted to be, but her separation anxiety—from me specifically—was so intense that I couldn't go to the bathroom without her maniacally clawing at the closed door and panting and pacing again.

Then Maybelline began resource guarding against my dogs—but the resource was the house itself, and sometimes my very body. While crated—which I was instructed to do for a couple of hours every day, so that she would be forced to manage being alone—she did everything to destroy the crate and her own face and paws. Though she was housetrained almost immediately upon arrival—she basically trained herself, just as she immediately learned "sit" and other basic obedience on the first command—she peed anxiously whenever left alone, either in her crate, in the car, or a closed room. By day five she was barking incessantly—at nothing. And by day seven she had bitten me as I carried my basenji past her to let my poor dog outside to pee.

While I fostered Maybelline, the SPCA came into possession of several more dogs from this particular household, so I learned more about her beginnings. It was a house with seventeen dogs living in it, while the human owners lived in an RV next door. The dogs were never let outside. They were fed inside in such a way that they had to compete and fight for their food. They were all intact—not "fixed"—and had interbred at will. As more of the females were confiscated, one ran away and was never seen again. Another had just had puppies, all of which had died. One was so feral she couldn't be touched. Maybelline herself, only a year old, had gray hairs on her face—from scarring, a sign of fighting.

Halfway through the week, when Maybelline had started attacking my dogs over space, I drove down to the shelter and said she should be placed with someone who has no other animals. But I was told there were no such fosters, and that I was her best bet. I had agreed to just one week, I said, my stomach turning with guilt and sadness. As I gave back all her things, including the snacks and toys I had bought her, the shelter asked if I would be willing to swap her out for the female whose puppies had just died. I was, by all accounts, a model dog owner, a valuable foster. The opposite of the people from whom these dogs had been taken.

And yet, I clearly wasn't. I couldn't handle it. Her resource guarding against my dogs was too much for me; I had to keep them safe in their own home. Like a helicopter parent, I so feared anything happening to them that I couldn't think straight about how to handle the situation. I returned home alone, beaten down by the whole experience and everything I should have done differently.

I was surprised by how fiercely I missed her. Here we were, the original owners and I—*the hoarders and I*—connected by this dog. I hoped the shelter was able to tell them that their dogs were safe and well cared for. I wished I could show them videos of Maybelline sitting for treats, going on long, ponderous leashed walks, and sleeping next to my head. I am absolutely sure that in their own way they wanted the very best for their dogs.

The tropes that animate *Confessions: Animal Hoarders* also animate shows about exemplary dog ownership. The most recent of these is *The Pack,* which premiered in 2020, basically a couples reality-TV, survivor-elimination show, except that the couples consist of dogs and their owners. The couples compete against each other in problem-solving challenges held in scenic locations around the world, in which their bond is showcased (and, as the script keeps reminding us, is strengthened by the show itself).

These are all fit, young professionals, most of them urban, rather than older folks living in low-income communities. The dogs are purebred and live the most charmed lives possible. The dyad—one dog, one human—is held up as the ultimate expression of dog ownership, which is remarkable in a show called *The Pack*. Despite its reliance on adventure content, the thrill of competition, and spectacular scenery, the show is both breathtakingly normal and normative. Everyone is perfect, a cohort of upwardly mobile young professionals that have overcome adversity with the help of man's best friend. And it's no small detail that they are competing for half a million dollars, in addition to hundreds of thousands to donate to a charity of their choice.

As spectacles of dog ownership, *Confessions: Animal Hoarders* and *The Pack* at first appear like they couldn't possibly be more different. And yet, the human-interest stories behind each couple in *The Pack* are very similar to those that *Animal Hoarders* uses to explain how this single, isolated person began hoarding. Trauma and loss—from deaths of unborn children to premature deaths of parents, from military PTSD to tragic deaths of former dogs, from childhood bullying to rock-bottom depression, addiction, and "starting over"—this, we discover, is how each of the people became so bonded with their one dog, the dog of their life, their "ride or die." Almost all the owners describe their dogs as their children, or as a buffer against the social pressure to find human partners and marry. And both shows tap into dog ownership as the true experience of living well with others, of intimacy, security, mutual support, interdependence—from friendship to family.

Is this a projection, a metaphor, a substitution? Is it a collective hallucination? Not exactly. Dogs were the first domesticated animal (the latest research dates this to 23,000 years ago[1]), and they accompanied humans as they dispersed throughout the world. Dogs have been an integral part of the social infrastructure in

---

1. Angela R. Perri, et. al., "Dog Domestication and the Dual Dispersal of People and Dogs into the Americas," *Proceedings of the National Academy of Science of the United States of America* 118, no. 6 (February 9, 2021), https://www.pnas.org/content/118/6/e2010083118.

which the human species came to flourish. They were not just in the margins of that flourishing; their specific forms of companionship contributed to it so actively that it would not be an exaggeration to say that there would be no humans as we know them without dogs. It's no surprise that dogs are considered part of the social unit, given that this is exactly what they have always been. Without any hint of substitution or projection, it may be said that human–dog relations are relations of love, and, as Donna Haraway writes in *When Species Meet,* "This love is a historical aberration and a naturalcultural legacy."[2]

But there is, at the same time, an intense and often deliberate substitution happening. Recent changes in dog-owner culture indicate that people are openly looking to dogs to help alleviate their increasing loneliness and disappointment with other people. The old adage that women who didn't or couldn't have children disappeared into life with animals is becoming simply, literally true, as birth rates all over the world fall and pet-adoption rates soar. The fear that dogs might simply replace children has reached as far as the Vatican, causing Pope Francis to criticize people who opt to have no children or who stop at one child but simultaneously adopt multiple cats or dogs. He claims that this turn away from children and toward animals "diminishes our humanity."[3]

While "my dog is my child" is unproblematically—even if a bit metaphorically—true without any extra context, it takes on a different kind of meaning when a hoarding older person makes it

2. Donna Haraway, *When Species Meet* (Minneapolis: University of Minnesota Press, 2007), 16.
3. Joshua Berlinger, "Opting for Pets over Children Is Selfish and 'Takes Away Our Humanity,' Says Pope Francis," *CNN,* January 5, 2022, https://www.cnn.com/2022/01/05/europe/pope-dogs-cats-kids-intl /index.html.

clear that her actual children don't visit her because they're too busy with their own lives. Or when a contestant on *The Pack* uses her dog as a buffer against invasive family members asking why she isn't married yet. This is a form of substitution, yes, but it's not just some silly misplacement of feelings. It's a deliberate turn away from humans and toward less toxic social relationships—with dogs. And though few would call most dog-hoarding cases instances of a healthy relationship, there's no denying that, no matter how unhealthy it may be for the dogs, it is nevertheless less traumatizing for the human hoarder than the company of her "fellow" humans.

I, too, have endured a tragedy. My beloved basenji Z, the first dog of my own I ever had, was taken from me brutally by the fire that burned down my boyfriend's house while we were working abroad, while our animals were in the care of a live-in dog sitter, our good friend. That person left the wood-burning stove on for the animals while he went to work, and something went wrong. We never found out exactly what. Along with my boyfriend's cat, Markybear, Z perished horribly, terrified and without her people, in the very same house where I, her one and only, had told her to stay and wait for me.

I die inside every time I think about it. There is no take on what happened that makes it bearable.

Z filled my heart so fully when she was still alive that it never occurred to me to want a second dog. Once she was gone, no number of dogs could numb my need, the ache to hold her once more, even just to comfort her while she died. It's been three years since the fire, but nothing helps, if I am honest. The love I feel for Abba and Waffles feels like it comes from another person than the person who loved Z, another life, another body. The person writing right now is not the same one who belonged to Z. And this new me is insatiable for dogs. I have entered a new world of dog ownership, one in which I must regularly curb my hunger for opening my doors ever wider to all the dogs in the world that need homes, a list that keeps growing longer.

I can no longer tell if it was Z herself that turned me inside out and opened me to other ways of knowing and loving, or if it was her loss that did this to me. She is and thus will always be the one that got away.

This is a little book about the oldest relationship that humans have cultivated with another large animal—something like the original interspecies space, as old or older than any other practice that might be identified as human. But it's also about the role of this relationship in the attrition of life in late capitalism. As we become more and more obsessed with imagining ourselves as benevolent rescuers of dogs, it's increasingly clear that it is dogs who are rescuing us. They are our flotation devices in a sea of precarity, not the other way around.

The Covid adoption craze is just one stage in a much longer process, which NPR now calls "the pet revolution." Dog ownership has been steadily on the rise since the 1990s. Dog food and other products are more expensive than ever, euthanasia rates have declined dramatically, and the pet industry keeps generating more and more jobs. The most probable reason for this sudden growth in pets in the late '90s has to do with the arrival of the internet: the attrition of traditional social relations and communities caused people to turn to dogs to fill the void.[4]

We are leaning on dogs more heavily than ever for the emotional labor of sustaining an unsustainable world. This form of

4. Greg Rosalsky, "How 'The Pet Revolution' Unleashed a New Top Dog in America," *NPR*, April 10, 2021, https://www.npr.org/sections/money/2021/08/10/1025596981/how-the-pet-revolution-unleashed-a-new-top-dog-in-america.

extraction lives in unexpected places—not only in actual dog–owner relationships, or even in the recently invented abstract category of "emotional support animal," but in TV shows, in presidential elections (Major Biden made national headlines as the first rescue dog in the White House), on TikTok, and even on our online dating profiles, where a photo with a dog increases one's appeal so much that people have begun "dogfishing," posing with dogs that aren't theirs.[5] Exactly what it is we are trying to "get" out of dogs is less and less clear.

Recently, an article by Margaret Renkl in the *New York Times* informed that, "In any household, the true master of hope is the family dog." But the description of the household in question, a middle-class, married suburbia straight of out Norman Rockwell—the new puppy, carefully placed with them by a rescue organization, makes everyone laugh with his crazy antics, like "stealing shoes from the shoe basket and hiding them around the house, grabbing the book I'm reading and running away with it, sneaking a sip of iced tea when my back is turned"[6]—situates this claim in a very specific mode of late-capitalist life. This is the mode in which dog articles in the mainstream media announce hopeful states, precisely because actual hope is in ever-shorter supply. Regardless of how fervently the author declares herself an optimist, the life and environment she describes, including the normative, predictable, and slightly infantilized role that her dogs seem to play in it—ultimately fail to inspire hope in the reader.

The article lacks any unique identifying characteristics for

5. Terry Nguyen, "Dogfishing: When Online Daters Pose with Adorable Pets That Aren't Theirs," *Washington Post,* August 12, 2019, https://www.washingtonpost.com/lifestyle/2019/08/12/dogfishing-when-online-daters-pose-with-adorable-pets-that-arent-theirs/.

6. Margaret Renkl, "Everything I Know about Hope I Learned from My Dog," *New York Times,* July 5, 2021, https://www.nytimes.com/2021/07/05/opinion/hope-dogs.html.

either dogs or people. It is instead a sort of catalog of indices of every dog's perfect America: squirrel chasing, dog biscuits tossed by UPS drivers, and "silly antics" like climbing bookcases to get food get food get food. During and after the pandemic lockdown, when people seemed to rediscover dog ownership and suddenly the media were abuzz about its advantages, articles like Renkl's, intended as intimate, down-home messages of optimism, inadvertently serve up blandness and lack of detail as defining features of life itself. There is no bigger message to turn to here. The result is that her claim that dogs are a source of hope begs the question: hope for what?

In what follows, I attempt to think about dogs and humans—the original and most emotionally intense interspecies relationship in human history—coexisting in late-capitalist captivity. Dogs are nothing less than the beating heart of the human condition, at once ancient and only just beginning to show itself. What is the relationship between our mutual captivation and the material and affective conditions that literally hold us captive, in very different but intimately related ways?

We live in dog-rich times. Canidae, the biological subfamily consisting of dog-like (as opposed to cat-like) carnivores, are the most abundant and adaptive mammals on earth, living on every continent except Antarctica. Out there, right at the edges of our collective political-economic captivity, is the wilderness, their wilderness, where wild canids rule. While so many apex predators are going extinct due to human presence, wild canids are thriving, in large part because they seem to adapt especially well to those same places where humans live. Coyotes, whose numbers are always on the rise and whose range continues to expand across the globe, especially thrive in cities.[7] Even as some

7. Patrick Pester, "How Did Coyotes Become Regular City Slickers?" *Live Science*, March 21, 2021, https://www.livescience.com/why-coyotes-in-cities.html.

wild dog species are verging on extinction—the African wild dog is one of the most endangered mammals on the planet—there are more canids alive, both wild and domesticated, than ever in history. Domesticated dogs are the world's most populous large animals, numbering around one billion, outnumbered only by factory-farmed livestock animals and the humans that create and destroy them.

As true wilderness recedes further out of reach, domestic dogs become our "windows on the disappearing wild," according to John McLaughlin in his book *The Canine Clan*.[8] He writes that, once all the intelligent wild mammals are gone, including primates and cetaceans, "we will be pretty much alone here. Whose mind will we share in that lonely time, only a few decades hence? Why, that of the dog, of course. Alone among comparable intelligences, his is likely to share the world with us for some time to come."[9]

But what does that sharing of the world actually look like? And is it still appropriate to describe this as a meeting of "intelligences"? Almost thirty years after McLaughlin wrote those words, dogs populate our social media, and not only in the already too-familiar manner of the Instagram influencer, but evermore weirdly, more and more TikTok videos showing a dog's last day or last meal before euthanasia. TikTok is also the theater for the training wars, conflicts among dog trainers about the best methods. Meanwhile, dog hoarding cases appear to be on the rise. Dog abundance is complicated in a world in which humans struggle more and more with social life, not only with doing it but with the question of what it even means anymore. And it seems that this sharing is no longer limited to the sphere of mind but

8. John McLaughlin, *The Canine Clan: A New Look at Man's Best Friend* (New York: Viking, 1983), xii.
9. McLaughlin, ix.

involves affects, and the technologies and institutions that shape affects—indeed, every institution governing life today.

This book is not a history of the myriad fraught ways that dog–human relations act as a theater for human-on-human violence, especially against people of color and poor people of all ethnicities. Excellent books on these topics already exist.[10] It's also not an engagement with one of the liveliest media topics of the moment, namely the true story of dog domestication, one that continuously changes as paleoanthropologists and geneticists pursue the topic hoping to arrive at a stable picture. It also doesn't explore different modes of canine–human relations that currently exist and are just as much direct products of late capitalism, except in the so-called developing world—most notably the abundance of street dogs and the eating of dogs.

It's overwhelming, writing about dogs. I'm sure that there is no such thing as a thinking that gets at "dogs in general." Dog being is too diverse, too ancient, too widespread, and humans are too intimately close to it to get critical distance or solid footing. On top of it all, as the best trainers will tell you, every individual dog is different. And finally, with dogs, one is never oneself: one is always in a state of being undone by them. One cannot think straight. Thinking-with-dogs must learn this as its first rule:

---

10. See Colin Dayan, *With Dogs at the Edge of Life* (New York: Columbia University Press, 2016), *The Law Is a White Dog* (Princeton, N.J.: Princeton University Press, 2013) and *Animal Quintet* (Los Angeles: Los Angeles Review of Books, 2020); Joshua Bennett's *Being Property Once Myself: Blackness and the End of Man* (Cambridge, Mass.: Harvard University Press, 2020); Bénédicte Boisseron's *Afro-Dog: Blackness and the Animal Question* (New York: Columbia University Press, 2018); Harlan Weaver's *Bad Dog: Pitbull Politics and Multispecies Justice* (Seattle: University of Washington Press, 2021); and Donna Haraway's *When Species Meet*, for a few titles that discuss dogs in relationship to settler colonialism, racism, and gender violence.

your thinking will necessarily outrun you, your emotions will be pulled out from under you by this relationship. As Barry Lopez famously wrote, "To be rigorous about wolves—you might as well expect rigor of clouds."[11]

But one does expect some things of clouds, even if not rigor. I have come to know and love the clouds where I live, and I ponder and photograph them on a regular basis. They are familiar. So I am binding myself here to the familiar, limiting myself to my particular situation, and answering a call I found in another book. In Colin Dayan's wise and deeply moving *With Dogs at the Edge of Life,* she writes: "If we were challenged to write a history of dispossession, we could go to no better place that the foreclosures of an imagined humanity when bounded and sharpened by the dog kind."[12] But Dayan herself seeks to set a mood rather than writing a history of dispossession. "Mood replaces certainty," she writes, nudging us into a different space of intelligibility.[13] My goal is to follow her invitation: to zero in on some aspects of the media ecosystem and social moment in which I find myself as a dog owner and -lover, and to map out the contours of that mood, the mood of a dispossession shared by my social context, which increasingly includes dogs.

Indeed, dogs require a different space of intelligibility, but not only because theirs is a different animal intelligence. My working hypothesis is that dogs belong to another mode of existence than the one the present demands of us. There is a movement in social studies of technology to shift focus from the "quantifiable self" to something more real, earthbound, embodied, what computer scientist and science writer Linda Stone calls "the essential self." This book could be understood as making the case that dogs are

11. Barry Lopez, *Of Wolves and Men* (New York: Scribners, 1976), 4.
12. Dayan, *With Dogs at the Edge of Life*, 3.
13. Dayan, xvi.

an "essential self technology."[14] The quantified self is the self that all the structures of late capitalism treat, from medicine to work to insurance (indeed, Stone sometimes calls this self "actuarial"). In contrast, the essential self is everything that exceeds what can be measured. This is precisely why thinking with dogs is a mood: we access the parts of ourselves that the endless attention to measurement cannot access, and the shift in psychophysical state is palpable. The true abundance that dogs have to offer is that of the unquantifiable—a right, if you will, to the essential self. This, I believe, is the source of the familiarity inside their strangeness, this return to the essential self that life with dogs opens onto, at least potentially.

Rather than pretend at objective evaluations, I've decided to embrace my obsession and speak from the perspective of the closeted hoarder, the one who wants too much, loves too hard, and probably does it wrong despite her best intentions—a limited, particular take generated by my own conditions of dispossession. Perhaps an alternative title for this introduction could have been "Confessions of a Cloud Chaser."

The following three chapters deal with three different aspects of social life as seen through the recent turn to dogs as both agents and subjects of rescue. In "Life," I examine the logics of rescue itself, the social imaginary that governs contemporary adoption procedures under biocapitalist logics of what it means to have a life. In "Food," I turn to work and eating, two dimensions central to slow death, or the idea that life under the capitalist regime is actually sucking the life out of us—dogs, humans, and indeed, the assemblage that is dogs-and-humans

14. Personal conversation, October 25, 2021. See also Linda Stone, "The Essential Self: Health beyond the Numbers," *Lindastone.net*, December 6, 2013, https://lindastone.net/2013/12/06/the-essential-self -health-beyond-the-numbers/.

in relation. In "Order," I consider the place of the pack model in how humans see life with others today. My suspicion is that all models for the dog-and-human assemblage are utopian, and so I ask us to consider what exactly we want from this relationship today, what deeper desires it answers. Each chapter offers an analysis of a cultural phenomenon and ends by zeroing in on one of the deeper questions that the phenomenon presents us. My goal is not to develop a "philosophy of dogs" but to show that living with dogs demands better, more careful thinking about life than what is currently available in philosophy.

Finding the true abundance that dogs offer the world means, first of all, pushing back against the false abundances, the ones that result in the bankruptcy of our inner lives and relationships, and even of our bodies. The ones that are really just scarcity, dressed up. We know that dogs make us better people, and, in doing so, make the world better. And yet, it seems, none of the existing structures that organize life allow for their thriving, which would in turn help human thriving. The life that dogs and humans could help each each other make has yet to emerge.

1. Life: "Adopt, Don't Shop" and the Terror of the Fence

WE ARE SURROUNDED—no, engulfed—by a rapidly growing and increasingly self-aware dog-owner culture. As Amanda Mull writes in her *Atlantic* piece, "Why Are Millennials So Obsessed with Dogs?" millennials have overtaken boomers as the largest pet-owning group in the country, and by some counts, more than half of them own a dog. "The pet-ownership rate is even higher among those with a college education and a stable income—the same people who are most likely to delay marriage, parenthood, and homeownership beyond the timelines set by previous generations."[1] But the ones who are buying homes are equally dog-crazy: a recent survey found that 33 percent of homebuyers gave their dog as the main reason for buying, outranking marriage and children as the incentive.[2] Dogs have become walking, breathing

1. Amanda Mull, "Why Are Millennials So Obsessed with Dogs?" *Atlantic,* July 29, 2021, https://www.theatlantic.com/magazine/archive/2021/09/why-millennials-are-so-obsessed-with-dogs/619489/.

2. Nicole Spector, "One Big Reason Millennials Are Buying Homes? For Their Dogs," *NBCnews.com,* August 9, 2017, https://www.nbcnews.com/business/real-estate/one-big-reason-millennials-are-buying-homes-their-dogs-n790921.

symbols of the good life—leading actors in fantasies of how we should live, whether those fantasies are normative or antinormative. Whether we are looking to hack late-capitalist captivity or we hope that conformity with it will bring the relief it promises, more and more and more of us are looking to dogs to "soothe the psychic wounds of modern life."[3]

The pandemic created new forms of social life—new isolations as well as new intimacies—and the current moment, in which we are under pressure to return to normal, means some difficult adjustments for dogs and for humans. Sharing a home with a dog became a microcosm for how much better life could be if people had more time and control over how they organize it. During quarantine especially, as families with children struggled to keep up with remote schooling and domestic partnerships suffered from the monotony of spending too much time in one space, relationships with dogs flourished and people reported enjoying quarantine much more as a direct result.[4] The disruption of business as usual provided a window into how different things could be, and dogs became the prime actors in that, a projection screen for the positive aspects of being "stuck at home" during the pandemic, as well as the unhappiness many people felt when forced to return to the office. One of the major rallying cries against returning to work has been the narrative about pandemic dogs being dumped in shelters in droves, which turned out to be fake news[5] but continues to inspire endless social media posts offering proof of how horrible human beings really are.

3. Mull, n.p.

4. Alexandra Horowitz, "Dogs, at least, Love Home Quarantine," *New York Times,* March 27, 2020, https://www.nytimes.com/2020/03/27 /opinion/coronavirus-dogs.html.

5. Michael Levenson, "No, People Are Not Returning Pandemic Dogs in Droves," *New York Times,* May 22, 2021, https://www.nytimes .com/2021/05/22/us/dog-adoptions-pandemic.html.

The discourse that presents pandemic dog ownership as if it were a universal human experience forgets that only a certain sector of the economy got to work from home and was later saddled with that unhappy office return. For nonessential workers, being "stuck at home" meant not only access to specific resources and spaces but also the upending/questioning of the work-centered lives they knew prior to Covid, that dramatic reshuffling of lifestyle and values we read about in the media. Suddenly the national conversation was asking *what really matters in life?* as a question for the upwardly mobile creative class.

But what was an opportunity to change our lives quickly became a means to reinforce existing middle-creative-class norms and expectations. As the demand for dogs grew, rescues, or nonprofits that are largely foster based rather than community shelters, were able to be more selective about who was allowed to adopt. Already famously difficult to work with, rescues became even more absurdly selective—and expensive.[6]

As rescue-dog content floods social media feeds, rescues pull all the most easily adoptable dogs from shelters, charge much higher fees for them than do shelters, and deem most potential adopters unworthy of purchasing one of their dogs. "Adopt, Don't Shop" started as a campaign against buying puppies from pet stores but has quickly morphed into a movement that argues that no one should get their dog from a breeder, no matter how responsible and well-heeled the breeder's operation. It forgets this important fact: rescues often stand in the way of what could be perfectly successful adoptions, imposing prohibitive, elitist requirements.

6. Allie Conti, "No, You Beg. Adopting Used to Be a Good Thing That Good People Could Do. These Days, You're Probably Not Good Enough," *The Cut,* July 29, 2021, https://www.thecut.com/2021/07/why -adopting-a-rescue-dog-is-so-hard-right-now.html.

"Adopt, Don't Shop" creates a false dichotomy between shelters and breeders, when in fact these two (if we take "breeders" to mean reputable, responsible animal-husbandry professionals who charge up to US$5,000 for a puppy, depending on breed and pedigree) represent two distant poles on a very large spectrum of ways that people get access to adoptable dogs. These include Craigslist, where backyard breeders sell their puppies for closer to $300–1,000 (though I once saw an exceptionally photogenic and small pug-mix puppy whose "rehoming fee" was $4,000). People hoping to rehome their dogs often post them on Craigslist rather than surrendering them to a shelter. And the remainder of that spectrum is taken up by different kinds of nonprofit animal rescue organizations, certainly if the desired dog is an adult and/or purebred.

The category "rescues" is broad and more diverse than I have space to explore. I will focus here on some similarities among them, rather than differences, and specifically on those similarities that ultimately result in the creation of the Acceptable Dog Owner, the one whose normative lifestyle matches them well with another creation, the Highly Adoptable Dog.

"Rescue dog" discourse—maintained by the "Dodo" on Facebook, rescue organizations on TikTok, and a long list of videos on YouTube—constructs fantasies of a depth of encounter that changes lives—of both the rescued and the rescuer. But working with a rescue is difficult and often leads nowhere. In the end, rescues reward the lifestyles that they recognize as worthy of maintaining a dog, and adoption is often contingent on proof that these lifestyles won't change. The difficulties of working with rescues lead many people to "shop" rather than adopting.

"Adopt, Don't Shop" usually rests on an imagined "us and them" dichotomy between two groups: entitled, young, rich Instagrammers who want golden retriever puppies and real folks like you and me who can waltz into a shelter to find an adult pitbull someone else surrendered and waltz out with it to go live happily ever after. Only the latter is morally acceptable: we, not they, are in it for the right reasons. But this binary doesn't reflect the reality very well, and in fact has some serious consequences. For one, it discourages people from adopting puppies across the board, without taking into account that some people, especially those with small children, have perfectly good reasons for wanting a puppy and not an adult dog. I might want a puppy if I have particularly active or loud kids (a bad match for most adult shelter dogs), or if I already own a dog-reactive dog (most adult dogs will not aggress on a puppy, while many have problems with other adult dogs entering the home). I keep meeting people who have bought puppies from breeders simply because their local shelter didn't have any: those highly adoptable puppies had been scooped up by rescues.

Rescues often will not release any dogs, including puppies, unless the potential owners agree to a home visit, provide access to the vet records of all animals living in the house, and bring all the animals' shots up to date. Some will not adopt out to people who rent rather than own their own home (and they require proof of ownership). Many require a fenced-in yard.[7] Meanwhile, buying a home is harder and more expensive than ever, and home ownership is becoming an outdated marker of a middle-class life that is quickly vanishing. Rescue applications reduce responsible dog ownership to economic status, which is mistakenly called "stability," as if anything economic could actually be stabilized in such precarious times.

But the problem isn't that the requirements are too difficult to meet. It is the very logic of these requirements, which reduces

---

7. Jennifer Billock, "Want to Adopt a Pet? Prepare for a Full Background Check," *New York Times*, June 22, 2021, https://www.nytimes.com/2021/06/22/style/pet-adoption-application.html.

the essential self to the quantified self,[8] that is the problem, since the quantified self is what we long to escape when we long for dogs. Unconditional love, the reason so many people cite for wanting or having dogs, lives in a different world than the one in which we keep up with the Joneses.

When it comes to adult dog adoption, the constraints are even stricter than those for puppies, since puppies are easily placed in a home with children, cats, and pretty much any other animal. I've spoken to many people who did not even especially want a puppy but felt forced to "shop" because when they applied for the adult dogs available through rescues, their applications were rejected. The local shelter was full of dogs that were either too big (a common problem in rural areas, where shelters are full of pit bull mixes, lab mixes, and shepherd mixes) or had come in with considerable behavioral issues with which less experienced adopters or those with small children rightly felt ill-equipped to deal. Meanwhile, most of the dogs on Petfinder.com who are in foster homes and belong to rescues won't be placed in homes with an existing dog. Rescues that allow for other dogs often specify exactly what kind of dog makes an appropriate match (gender, age, size, and activity level are often specified and non-negotiable).

Like the adoption of human children via agencies, dog adoption via rescues is not something everyone can afford. While you should expect to pay between $100 and $200 for a dog at your local shelter, rescues often charge from $300 upwards for a healthy dog. Those that specialize in purebred dogs, especially showy breeds like afghan hounds or borzoi, can charge up to

8. Wade Roush, "Linda Stone's Antidote to the Quantified Self: The Essential Self," *xconomy.com,* August 8, 2014, https://xconomy.com /national/2014/08/08/linda-stones-antidote-to-quantified-self-the -essential-self/.

$900 per dog. The average price of a dog through a nonprofit rescue (rather than a shelter) on Petfinder seems to be around $500. While the intensely sentimental texts that accompany the photos ask, "Could you find room in your home and heart for me?" the real but unspoken question is "Can you afford me?"

The justification for the price is the belief that only people who can afford regular vet care should own dogs. If you can't afford the rescue price tag, the logic goes, how can you afford to take care of your dog for the rest of its life? But this argument misses one important fact about money: when it's scarce (which it usually is these days), people tend to prioritize. It also misses the cultural and individual differences between people when it comes to imagining what one can and cannot afford. For example, I come from a family where a massage is considered the height of extravagance. The point is not that I can't actually afford a massage, but that it's the last thing I would buy for myself, in part because I am always aware of how my money "should be" allocated. And in a country with such minimal social services as the United States, one of the things I know very well I absolutely have to save for is the rainy day, the emergency. In other words, I am the epitome of a person who *both* balks at the $700 price tag on the dog I long to adopt *and* the person who saves precisely so that she can afford her vet bills. There is no contradiction there, and just because I wouldn't pay the $700 for the rescue dog does not mean that I cannot afford to pay for the vet. An emergency visit to my local vet—Abba recently had a temperature, required bloodwork and multiple medications to fight off a tick-borne infection, for example—costs roughly that much, in fact.

Which brings me to the people who actually cannot afford veterinary care. They are the ones that could most benefit from owning a dog, the ones who are not enjoying economic stability. Data show extraordinary success with the introduction of dog programs into just about any "at risk" population. Prison animal programs across the country are thriving and boast much lower recidivism among inmates who worked with animals in training programs. Dog-training programs are being introduced into rehabilitation for at-risk youth, and therapy dogs are actively at work in long-term care facilities like nursing homes. Service dogs famously help with everything from PTSD to addiction. The long-term effects of sustained interaction with a dog—i.e., a relationship—bring statistically proven improvements to people's lives, especially lives that are full of stress, anxiety, instability, trauma, and loneliness.

We might ask: How are dogs supposed to help turn us into better people if we must already be close to perfect to be allowed to adopt?[9] How are they to bring out our best qualities when the adoption process negates the differences among us and works in favor of a social monoculture? When it reduces us to our paychecks and ignores our potential to turn our lives around?

Anytime there is a mainstream conversation unfolding around what really matters in life—and the Covid era has certainly been a moment for that—dogs feature prominently in the discussion. They become a projection screen for how very different life could be, and indeed, adoption stories focus on the life-changing aspects of introducing a dog into one's life. Simultaneously, however, dog-adoption practices are framed strictly by a particular version of what it means to have a life at all, one that hardly deviates from existing norms or calls for people to imagine anything the least bit different. The more scarce dogs become—as happened during the Great Adoption of 2020—the stricter the rules we have to follow to be deemed worthy of adopting.

Mull continues, "For people clawing to maintain basic stability

9. Susan Pinker, "Do Dogs Really Make Us Happier?" *Wall Street Journal,* December 30, 2020, https://www.wsj.com/articles/do-dogs -really-make-us-happier-11609348272.

(instead of signaling that they've attained a middle-class version of it), the barriers to dog ownership are larger than simply having the disposable income to feed another mouth. A lot of subsidized and low-income housing refuses pets or limits the type and number that residents can have, and homeless shelters generally require people to abandon their pets to get a place to sleep. Companionship, whether with a pet or other people, is elemental to human dignity; in America, it's easier to come by if you have money."[10] Rescue adoption applications are clearly looking for those signals of having arrived and won't settle for less.

The outdated expectation that an adopter be a "stable," middle-class homeowner leaves many people with only shelters or Craigslist to adopt from. The "rescue" logic that discriminates against people who don't wish to spend many hundreds of dollars up front on a dog actually sends many of those folks to Craigslist, where they can pay $100 for a cute pittie puppy from a backyard breeder, thus continuing the cycle of backyard breeding that lands so many pitbulls in shelters and ultimately killed. Shelters are full of dogs that have been adopted and quickly returned, multiple times. Rescues like to blame this high return rate on adopters not being vetted properly. But the actual cause is the complete lack of support for those people who want dogs but can't work with a rescue because they don't meet the minimum requirements.

Such an abandoned dog is likely to have behavioral difficulties like resource guarding (including food aggression), separation anxiety, or high anxiety in general, which might result in biting or running away—problems that most people don't wish or don't have the time to deal with. When adopters are rejected by rescues or simply wish to follow the imperative to prioritize dogs from

10. Mull, n.p.

their local shelter, they often end up with dogs that are actually much higher maintenance. And the longer a dog stays at the shelter, the more pronounced its behavioral problems become. It is these dogs that run the risk of eventually being declared a danger to shelter staff and being euthanized.

My own experience of trying to adopt a second basenji so that Abba might have a playmate has thus far been a total bust. The one existing basenji rescue organization in the United States, Basenji Rescue and Transport (BRAT), has complete, exhaustive control over every purebred basenji that needs rehoming in the country. Their network is nationwide, volunteer-run, and donation-based, and they are very good at what they do—unless, like me, you have been trying for years to adopt an adult basenji from them. In many ways, I am the perfect adopter for this particular breed, which is notoriously not-great with children, demanding, destructive, active, curious, and drawn to other dogs of the same breed (over other kinds of dogs). I have no children; I live in the country and spend much of my time outdoors; I work from home; and I am a basenji fancier, obsessed with the breed's history, looks, and quirks. I am basenji experienced and have the time and patience to work at helping a traumatized dog adjust. But I am missing one feature without which BRAT will never rehome a healthy, adult dog to me: a fence.

The terror of the fence, as I like to call it, is prevalent in rescue ads for many dogs, especially ones labeled active or "escape artists." Entire breeds have been branded as dogs that bolt and will not come when called (basenjis and beagles, for example). But such demands seem to forget that what one is really supposed to do with a dog is walk it. When I adopted my first basenji, my first dog ever and the dog of my heart, I lived on a busy city street in Baltimore. She was given to me because, after multiple rehomings, she could not even stay in the multi-dog kennel in which she had ended up. We fell in love. I walked Z on lead every time she had to go to the bathroom—four, sometimes five times a day. Z did not have a fenced yard, but she didn't need one. Had she been up for adoption through BRAT, I would have had zero chance. Their requirements effectively eliminate the segments of the population that wish to have a dog because they actually want to walk with it and not simply let it out to go to the bathroom.

Some people will argue that the fenced yard allows the dog to run and romp off-lead, while a leash walk doesn't. And that's true, of course, except that most dogs are not that interested in their immediate yards. When they run away from yards, it's precisely because they are bored there. The fence simply serves to keep in your bored dog, a literal tool of captivity. When it comes to off-lead walks, those should take place in some nature space that's relatively free of other dogs and humans, and they are opportunities to work on recall, training your dog to come when called. (Some breeds, like greyhounds, and some individual dogs have prey drive so strong that walking them off lead is never advised. But this is something that any owner in tune with their dog's personality and needs will be able to assess.)

Rescues celebrate the fence as the answer to the fleeing dog, when the real answer lies in spending time with and exercising your dog, with particular attention to training that ensures their safety. Really taking your dog out is the exact opposite of what fencing encourages. Fenced enclosures are great infrastructure for dog owners, among the many things that make owning a dog easier, but they are hardly signs of responsible, engaged ownership, which is how many rescues treat them.

Given BRAT's stranglehold on adult basenji adoption, a fenceless person like me has two choices: to completely give up on having a second dog of this breed or to shop, spending at least $2,000 on a puppy, when I would in fact prefer an adult (and so would Abba, who is a senior). I have now trial-adopted several dogs from the local shelter but was forced to return them when they showed aggression towards one or the other of my dogs, usually over a resource like space, a toy, or even access to me. But a basenji in foster care that has been vetted and declared not a threat to other dogs in the house is rare, and such rare dogs will only go to desirable owners, namely those with fences.

I have no doubt that BRAT and other rescues' fence requirement has in fact protected countless dogs from running away and potentially getting hurt and even killed. But staying alive does not make for a life, certainly not for creatures as profoundly embodied as dogs. To treat fences as a minimum requirement of responsible dog ownership is to forget that what dogs bring to our lives is that they take us away from home, from what we—and they—already know. A fenced yard is not to be confused with the outdoors, or with a dog's running and romping, which is in fact necessary to their physical and mental development. I would argue that it is also necessary to human development: at the precise moment when our time on earth is spent in relation to screens, dogs not only bring us back to our bodies but our bodies back to their environments.

Such profound confusions abound in every aspect of contemporary dog ownership, where a dog's (and their human's) basic needs for the outdoors, stimulation, closeness, shelter, and safety—an infrastructure that is as much psychological as it is physical—are consistently translated into consumer goods and services, from gear to professional training.

To be clear, my critique of rescues is not based in the belief that "it shouldn't be this hard" to adopt a dog. I absolutely believe there should be standards for adopting dogs but not at all the ones that presently rule the rescue scene. We can develop standards for adoption that turn the focus away from some idealized vision of the kind of home and family in which a dog is an appropriate addition to focus instead on dogs as a key to inner life and personal growth. Friendship, acceptance, physical affection, and more time spent outdoors, more mindful living—these are the rewards dogs bring to our lives, around which adoption must be reframed.

Could Living with Dogs Change the Stakes of Living?

Working from home under Covid restrictions led many of us to question what we have sacrificed for our professional lives and if it was indeed worth it. That was an exhilarating moment: when the Great Adoption met the Great Resignation. But what have we answered? In the United Kingdom, dog owners demanded that they be allowed to bring their dogs to the office, once in-person operations resumed. Some employers agreed to this, citing once again the optimized workplace in which dogs provide benefits to mental health and morale, bringing the "team" closer together.[11] Working dogs can finally become real nine-to-fivers, the whole team happily working together to increase profits. So far, it's considered a feature of the rapidly changing office environment. But does bringing my dog to the office not also mark a change in the relationship between dog and owner, a shift in how humans imagine reasons to adopt dogs in the first place?

Not even the pandemic can dislodge the power that the optimized life has on the contemporary upwardly mobile imagination. Dogs are the most significant nonhuman actors in this imaginary, as indicators of their human's financial stability, capacity for relationships (as major players in online dating profile pics), and other desirable traits, from maturity to connectedness with nature. The idea that all dogs are working dogs is sadly

11. Lucy Campbell, "Many New Dog Owners in UK Hope to Bring Pet into Work as Lockdown Eases," *Guardian*, July 12, 2021, https://www .theguardian.com/lifeandstyle/2021/jul/12/new-dog-owners-hope-pets -office-welcome-home-alone.

correct, but this feature is not some innate characteristic. It has emerged from the long and complex processes of canine domestication, yes, but this is only part of the story. Canine domestication has happened alongside the domestication of humans—indeed, their captivity—on a massive scale, a process in which everything that is alive in us must be put to work, in service of "the economy."

The tighter our bonds with dogs become and the less people question the place of dogs in homes and families, the more we use dogs to buttress existing structures and institutions, rather than allowing life with dogs to help us change them. The recent rise in businesses that allow landowners to rent their land to dog owners by the hour—the most visible of these is Sniffspot, the "Airbnb for dogs"—is an interesting example. Airbnb itself is under constant attack for its impact on housing stock, prices, and communities. How long before studies measure the impact of people buying land in order to turn it into private dog parks for those who can afford it?

In her wonderful memoir *Never Leave the Dog Behind,* poet Helen Mort writes, "All creatures change your habits."[12] She means this on the microlevel—the most banal, quotidian habits of the individual person—and she is absolutely right. It's interesting then that the individual changes don't add up to changes on the level of culture. Instead, humans project the very same cultural and economic structures that bring such misery onto dogs, or onto the social units that now include dogs. On the macrolevel, not only are we not changed by creatures, it seems, but it is we who change them. A revolutionary result of Covid could have been the realization that universal healthcare must include veterinary care, if we are serious that dogs are our family members,

12. Helen Mort, *Never Leave the Dog Behind* (Sheffield, UK: Vertebrate Publishing, 2020), 10.

and if we recognize the need to make dog ownership more affordable and thus accessible to everyone. Instead, we invented Airbnb for dogs.

The more dogs we adopt, the closer we get to dogs, the more we become aware of and attracted to their undeniable vitality—but this is also true for the forces of advanced capitalism, which seek out life and feed on it. When Colin Dayan writes about her love for dogs, I read her as commenting on this vitality. She is especially concerned with the figure of life, in questions like "How do I seize on dog life in words?" But the point here as I take it isn't just that dogs don't have words or that existing language misses the mark in expressing dog life. It's that the vitality of dogs makes humans confront not just dog life but life in general, in more and deeper ways. The question might as well read *How can I seize on life in words?*—the human question par excellence.

"These dogs changed my life. I wondered how I had lived all those years in New York without dogs, without their breath on my face and their warmth in my bed."[13] This passage struck home especially strongly, because I, too, lived in New York for some years and now feel like the time I spent without dogs as an adult was time "wasted," time I should have spent with dogs. As Mort puts it, "There are two types of people in this world: those who love dogs and those who haven't spent enough time with them yet."[14] During my New York years, I was simply one of the latter, not yet one of the former, but it's a version of myself I can barely remember anymore. Dogs make you forget who you were before you knew them.

Dayan continues, "Nothing mattered to me like these dogs. No man could be as close, no eyes as vivid, no flesh as neces-

13. Dayan, 44.
14. Mort, 13.

sary. . . . Never had I known anything incorruptible, so strong and blooded." And of course, no meditation on how profoundly dogs affect us in life is complete without continued astonishment at how much their deaths knock us off balance. "I sometimes wondered why they meant more to me than anything I had ever known before and why their deaths were to be remembered with all the stillness of worship, with an immensity of regret I never could muster for any human, not my parents, not for anyone I ever knew."[15]

It *is* astonishing that the grief is breathtakingly profound, for reasons no one can conclusively explain. But maybe the explanation is actually quite simple, and Dayan's book brings it into relief with its focus on dog life. We go on about unconditional love and losing our best friend, but maybe the reason that these tropes fail to describe the experience, that language itself fails and lands us in platitudes, has to do with how profoundly alive dogs are in life. When Z was wrenched from me, brutally and prematurely, there was something about the loss of her that reeked unmistakably of the loss of life itself, of my hard-won, vulnerable connection to a life that hadn't yet been fully coopted, stolen, fenced in, spoken for. I had lost her, my one and only, but I had also lost a bit of life itself that I would never get back.

If indeed dogs connect us to our essential selves, they do so in the way they do best: as beings highly sensitive to their environment and exquisitely socially evolved. They show us by example that the essential self is not a discrete, enclosed thing but is embedded in sociality and place, continuously transformed by encounters. "Dogself" exists entirely thanks to its surrounds and supports, which means that the dog life of which we speak is not just a force inside of dogs, animating them. It is also that

15. Dayan, 45.

thing to which they constantly direct our attention when we walk them: the living planet, the maddeningly thick, sensory world, with all its others. Much, and perhaps all, of this has to do with how much dogs are guided by smell, a sense unlike any other. In *The Mushroom at the End of the World,* Anna Lowenhaupt Tsing describes smell as a "combination of ineffability and presence."[16]

> Smell, unlike air, is a sign of the presence of another, to which we are already responding. Response always takes us somewhere new; we are not quite ourselves anymore—or at least the selves we were, but rather ourselves in encounter with another. Encounters are, by their nature, indeterminate; we are unpredictably transformed. Might smell, in its confusing mix of elusiveness and certainty, be a useful guide to the indeterminacy of encounter?[17]

From within life with dogs, the essential self means a self so embedded, so alert, directed, and in-communication, that the distinction between self and world pretty much disappears. No wonder they sleep so much.

It's no surprise, then, that dog ownership should become the site of discriminatory, exclusionary infrastructure, fantasies of moral purity, and a useful tool for enforcing all of the terrors on which extractive capitalism feeds. The Pope is not wrong when he calls the pet revolution a threat to our humanity, if we mean the kind of humanity that existing extractive systems need in order to survive. At stake is the most important thing: reality, life, the self, the planet. It's no wonder that every aspect of living with dogs, from the law to the imagination, is heavily policed, probably more so now than ever.

16. Anna Lowenhaupt Tsing, *The Mushroom at the End of the World* (Princeton, N.J.: Princeton University Press), 43.

17. Tsing, 46.

2. Food: The Working Dog and the Invention of Enrichment

"THE DOG WHISPERER," Cesar Millan's enormously popular TV show, which ran on National Geographic from 2004 until 2012, popularized the idea that all dogs, not just working breeds or those that actually assist in police, military, or medical jobs, want first and foremost to work for the rewards of food and human affection. Today the idea that all dogs naturally want to work is a commonplace. Banking on it, much of the advertising around pet products has come to rely on one of two fantasies: that of a golden age before domestication, when wolves roamed the earth and howled, far off in the distance, or that of a golden age of domestication, when early dogs and early humans lived side-by-side in harmony, hunting and eating together. This romantic imagery seems to have the strongest hold on dog food and feeding practices.

The basic tenet of the new lifestyle called work-to-eat is that placing a full food bowl at the dog's feet twice a day wastes an excellent opportunity to make the dog work for its meal, as all dogs originally had to do when they hunted alongside humans. Accordingly, the increasingly popular lifestyle calls for a new generation of interactive dog feeders. Encouraging owners to "banish the bowl," feeders like the Kong Wobbler release dog food over time, often requiring problem solving. This claims to improve dogs' lives in several areas: it slows down a dog that eats too fast and, more generally, it tires out the dog. There are recipes online for what to fill your Kong with, and many recommend freezing the filled Kong before giving it, so as to make the food even more difficult to obtain.

Proponents of work-to-eat claim that dogs who do not have to work for food are bored and potentially destructive. One website even compares domesticated dogs—in contrast to wild dogs and wolves—to workers who have retired too early, who have higher mortality rates and waste away in nursing homes.[1] Descriptions of feeders focus on how the dog will be challenged and stimulated, both mentally and physically, by the awkwardly shaped, mysterious plastic or rubber thing from which it must extract its meal, and occasionally describe the dog as "earning" its dinner.

Like many other new dog toys on the market, which have stopped resembling children's toys and cuddly stuffed animals, interactive feeders have distinctly minimalistic/futuristic design and are clearly meant to appeal to owner aesthetics. Their sleek, neutral looks fit well with not only the actual look of "the contemporary home," but also with how owners imagine an optimized life—for dogs as well as humans.

But the challenges that the work-to-eat lifestyle makes available to today's pet dogs have little in common with the meaningful work that created the idea of the dog as a worker in the first place.

Dogs were indeed fellow workers—who might have been said to "earn" something—but only because they had real jobs, tasks that accomplished much more than just exercising their minds

1. https://www.schoolforthedogs.com/puzzles-for-dogs-and-why-they-matter-98048/.

and muscles in order to get tired. These tasks were the key to dogs becoming our essential companions over millennia. The dramatic differences among dog breeds that exist today result-ed directly from human communities needing different things from the dogs who lived alongside them in particular regions, climates, and economic conditions. The specific jobs of dogs, like sled pulling, livestock herding, and hunting, were essential to community infrastructure. In warring cultures, dogs were used in fighting. To this day, dogs are irreplaceable experts when it comes to search and rescue, since no technology that can com-pete with a dog's sense of smell. The same goes for a service dog's ability to detect when someone is about to have a seizure, when their blood sugar is dangerously high, and in their ability to detect cancer—and now even Covid—by smell.

The commodification of dogs in the practice of breeding and its place in the history of agribusiness is hardly innocent, as Haraway has deftly pointed out.[2] But its history shows, at the very least, that it was the particular jobs—and not just the act of "keeping busy" itself—that mattered. This includes the invisible labor of females doing the reproductive work, in communities where prized puppies were traded for goods.

The work-to-eat concept has little connection with the real history of the working dog, or the dog as worker, who had a specific, important job to do and so was an essential part of the functioning of the community. Instead, today's pet owners are encouraged to offer their dogs maximum challenge and stimu-lation for its own sake, as if they were helping their dog become the best dog it could be. A tired dog, we are constantly told, is a good dog.

What is at stake in this idea—sometimes also called "enrichment"—and whom does it benefit?

2. Haraway, 53.

The term *enrichment* was originally applied to wild animals in captivity. Zoos and aquaria have environmental/behavioral enrichment programs that purport to increase the quality of life for their captive animals, providing species-specific stimuli to increase optimal psychological wellbeing. The goal is to counteract stereotypy, or phenotypic behaviors that are repetitive and maladaptive, serving no apparent goal. The classic zoo examples are caged animals pacing or swimming in circles, elephants swinging their trunks, and bar biting and excessive licking. Many of these cause harm to the animal.

In more domesticated contexts, examples of stereotypy include overgrooming in cats, dogs chasing their tails, and even hand flapping in humans. One of the animals most prone to stereotypies is the horse, with repetitive stall walking, weaving, crib biting, and wind sucking. These behaviors were once called abnormal because they are maladaptive. Today, however, they are taken to indicate abnormality not in the animal but in its environment. Enrichment was born within a specific framework—the need to provide psychologically damaged or otherwise stressed captive animals with mental stimulation. In other words, it is itself a symptom.

Animals with stereotypies have been shown to respond well to positive reinforcement training (PRT), where they are rewarded (usually with food) for doing certain tasks. For this reason, positive reinforcement and enrichment are categories that have grown together in the popular imagination. Enrichment toys are a key part of the general shift to positive reinforcement training in dog-owner culture. These are things that were once called toys but are now packaged as puzzles, problems to solve, or just mental "work," like sniff work. Tugging is also a popular reward for dogs that like to tug but are not sufficiently "food motivated."

Once more, however, this work has little to do with the jobs that working dogs once had. Enrichment in the form of "work" seems like nothing more than keeping your dog busy, a classic example of alienated labor, effort completely devoid of all of those powerful affective signs that social animals need to feel connected and important, signs that one's work actually matters to the successful functioning of a community or even the smallest social unit.

As devastating as alienated labor is for the human psyche, we should expect it to be even more damaging to dogs, who are social animals in much more literal ways than humans. "Social animal" doesn't just mean enjoying the company of others: it means constant cooperation for the sake of survival. One of the big lessons of positive reinforcement training is that food isn't the only motivator in training. Many dogs are actually more motivated by their beloved toy, or a game of tug, or even just praise and physical affection—whatever reinforces the relationship with their handler. The work isn't necessarily about food at all, except in the much deeper and more abstract sense that the dog seeks a closer and more functional relationship with its human. What this means is that the dog's willingness to work is product of interaction with humans, and not simply an extension of their ancestral wolves' natural hunting instincts. A dog undergoing PRT isn't hunting for the treat it receives as a training reward. It's solidifying its relationship with the social unit that will eventually go hunt and eat large prey together, protect territory and young, and work together to ensure thriving.

Neither is the dog earning its food. A dog doesn't earn food by eating it from a Kong any more than a human earns food by working out at the gym or wearing a FitBit. As with other lifestyles evoking a happier, healthier, more natural past, like the paleo diet, barefoot running, or earthing[3] work-to-eat relies

3. https://www.earthing.com/.

on broad, often superficial claims about animal instincts and reductive versions of the complicated histories of land, animals, and humans.

Although we imagine dogs as fundamentally food motivated, much more driven by appetite than humans, the concept behind this lifestyle is grounded at least as much in the history of human work culture as by what we know about canine nature. The phrase "work to eat" has no original connection to dogs. It first appears in the New Testament, 2 Thessalonians 3:10, where the aphorism "he who does not work, neither shall he eat" is at the heart of a moral condemnation of idleness, long considered a sin. Attributed to Paul the Apostle, the aphorism was cited in speeches by John Smith to the colony at Jamestown, Virginia, in the 1600s, and then by Lenin during the Russian Revolution in the early 1900s, and eventually the Soviet constitution of 1936.[4]

This ancient ethic is receiving a new lease on life today, with the shift from humans to dogs but also, and perhaps most importantly, with its emphasis on gear. The work-to-eat lifestyle is more reminiscent of a Silicon Valley startup buying standing desks or balance-ball chairs for its employees in order to enhance productivity. I have to work to be able to afford the latest gear to then be more productive at work.

The success of Kongs and other such feeders is due in part to the fact that they deliver on their promise of tiring your dog. They are especially useful for dogs that eat their food too quickly or dogs that are highly aroused or anxious—states that are often associated with and present in dogs that have been through scarcity in some form, whether it was being weaned too early or abandoned, or actually hungry, or simply in the presence of

4. Roland Boer, "The Bible and the Soviet Constitution of 1936," *Political Theology Network,* April 18, 2015, https://politicaltheology.com /the-bible-and-the-soviet-constitution-of-1936/.

resource guarding or reactive dogs in the shelter. When reduced to their most basic concept, interactive feeders are actually quite brilliant tools. Solving a puzzle not only tires out your dog but actually slows down their mind, a key component to counteracting anxiety or hyperactivity, functioning in a similar way to a walk. As one small part of a complex program to build a dog's confidence and mental balance, they are quite useful.

But context is everything. It is by no means obvious that, by itself, pulling kibble out of a puzzle feeder makes for a better, happier, richer dog life—unless we accept that today's "innovative" technologies and gear designs harness and cultivate strengths and talents that would otherwise remain forever hidden, like the perfect posture that improved office ergonomics promises to deliver. We would then have to further accept that the best world is one in which those hidden talents are put to use improving productivity. The goal in such a world is no longer just work but the optimizing of work and of life itself. And the sin in question is no longer sloth but allowing abilities to remain dormant when there are technologies available that would effectively put them "to work."

This distinctly advanced-capitalist way of thinking about work—in which everything is in its service—leads to exhaustion. And indeed, from far enough away, work-to-eat appears as a study in ongoing, mutual exhaustion between dogs and humans. The most positive user reviews of interactive feeders mention that the dogs are exhausted after using the product, an unquestioned positive in a world of dog ownership where humans are short on time and energy to devote to their dogs because of—you guessed it!—work. There are many other things that humans can do to use innovative feeding techniques in their training, like banishing feeding times altogether and reinforcing (by feeding by hand) only those behaviors one wants to see, like calm states, sitting, lying down, and during structured walks. Or keeping to feeding times but only hand feeding. But both of these require time and attention that working humans rarely have to devote to their dogs.

The Kong has simply replaced the bowl as that which we put in front of our dogs, hoping it will keep them busy. Feeding dogs from bowls has come under attack only recently, in the context of the other pressures of modern life in which dog owners must constantly look for new ways to tire out their dogs, for whom they never have quite enough time. Just because dogs are domestic animals doesn't mean they're not also in captivity. But just because dogs are "ours" doesn't mean that we're not also in captivity. And as the nonhuman animal closest to humans, dogs suffer alongside humans, their bodies and lives shaped thoroughly by the very same material and ideological conditions.

How Should We Feed Our Dogs?

Haraway was right to invoke Marx and Foucault in *When Species Meet*, in order to think about dog subjectivity and history. But today it's no longer just labor and biocapitalism that shape dog life: there are also patterns of "slow death" that apply directly to the shapes contemporary dog life is taking. Lauren Berlant's well-worn phrase refers to patterns in which "life building and the attrition of life are indistinguishable."[5] It's no accident that her classic essay is about agency—an important concept in any discussion of behavior and training—and food. More precisely, it's about obesity—the rhetoric and semiotics around its structural causes and proposed solutions. It's also no accident that dogs suffer from obesity in ever larger numbers. According to

5. Lauren Berlant, "Slow Death (Sovereignty, Obesity, Lateral Agency)," *Critical Inquiry*, special issue "On the Case," ed. Lauren Berlant, 33, no. 4 (Summer 2007): 754.

the AKC, in 2018 56 percent of American dogs were obese,[6] and pet obesity is currently described in the exact same language as human obesity, that of the epidemic.

At the heart of the dog–human relationship is food. It shapes the story of the original domestication of canids: humans killed more than they ate, thus becoming a source of food for dogs after the hunt. A new theory even claims that wolves were domesticated because early humans could not eat the large amounts of meat that were available after the hunt, thus leaving meat for wolves. It's an argument against the "paleo" diet, showing that early humans in fact ate a much more diversified diet than that fad recommends.[7]

But today, it's not at all clear what follows from this well-rehearsed fact of humans and dogs sharing food. To try to understand the enormously complex thing that goes under the innocent name "dog food" one must disaggregate a bunch of rhetorically and semiotically different kinds of agency and infrastructure. As Berlant writes, about humans, "the image of obesity as a phenomenon improvised by biopolitical experts needs to be separated from eating as a phenomenological act and from food as a space of expressivity as well as nourishment."[8] As more and more dogs become classified as obese, in the domain of biopolitical expertise, dog life will call for an ever-closer look

6. Susan Paretts, "How to Tell If Your Dog Is in Shape or Overweight," American Kennel Club website, August 7, 2019, https://www.akc.org/expert-advice/health/how-to-tell-if-your-dog-is-fat/.

7. Rachel Nuwer, "Dog Domestication May Have Begun Because Paleo Humans Couldn't Stomach the Original Paleo Diet," *Scientific American*, January 7, 2021, https://www.scientificamerican.com/article/dog-domestication-may-have-begun-because-paleo-humans-couldnt-stomach-the-original-paleo-diet/.

8. Berlant, 777.

at the complexity of food and the many critical frameworks and investigative methods it demands.

Work-to-eat appears to be about dogs but is actually another trend anchored in narratives about a happier, healthier, and more natural human past, simultaneously and surreptitiously designed to increase productivity and enhance performance in service of economic growth. It claims to banish the bowl because it's fundamentally "unnatural" for dogs, but the real reason is complicated by projections and fantasies about human nature and optimized life. Unsurprisingly, the company Varram has introduced a smart interactive feeder/fitness robot that promises to play with the dog in the owner's absence and dispense treats.[9] The company claims that incorporating such a robot into the human's busy lifestyle helps counteract their dog's lethargy and depression. Separation anxiety is a hot topic in the product's Amazon reviews, with owners claiming that they can finally leave the house because their dog is focused on the robot and not them. The human can finally go to work!

The appearance of such a product on the scene says much less about the past of dogs than it does about the future of humans. If indeed we want more meaningful relationships with our happier, healthier dogs, we must first interrogate our fantasies around work, productivity, and functionality, and their relationship to health and unhealth. No amount of gear can save us, not even when that gear is packaged as un-gear, a form of freedom from the stuff we used to buy and use that is now, we are told, obsolete.

How should we feed our dogs? is thus a real question. That there's no obvious answer indicates that we are facing the beating heart of something, a mystery as murky as the very origins of domestication itself. The point is not that we should stop

9. https://varram.com.

looking for answers but that all our answers are invariably shot through with our very human, very historically situated desires. How I should feed my dog depends in large part on how I imagine the relationship, what I want from it, how I evaluate it as more or less successful. What is the good life with dogs? What kind of life do I want to facilitate for them, and why? What do I want for them? These are the metalevel questions in which any answer about feeding will necessarily be couched. And it will take extraordinary vigilance to keep them safe from invasion by late-capitalist logics of the optimal.

3. Order: The Persistence of the Pack

I DON'T REMEMBER WHEN alpha theory was debunked. For most of us amateur dog enthusiasts (loving and dedicated owners who follow training tips closely but are not themselves professional trainers) it didn't explode like some epic singular event. Instead, as new trainers with new terminology came on the scene, we found out, bit by bit, that we could stop trying to be the "pack leader" we'd been hearing about for so long. What we are only now coming to realize is that the alpha paradigm has been scientifically discredited for decades. It lived on—and continues to live in the minds of many owners—thanks not to science but entertainment. Alpha theory wasn't introduced in the 2000s— the theory of the dominance hierarchy had been around since the 1940s, in research about wolves—but that's when it became a staple of every dog owner's vocabulary and conceptual scheme, thanks to *The Dog Whisperer.*

From 2004 to 2012, Cesar Millan's show brought dog training before American audiences like no other program, before or since. It became National Geographic channel's number one show during its first season and was broadcast in over eighty countries worldwide. Millan went on to write three *New York*

Times bestsellers and produce an empire of products, including a magazine for dog owners, a live lecture series, training tools, and a line dog food sold in most major grocery stores.

Millan's was a training grounded in dominance, but we didn't know that. We didn't have a name for it, because there was no alternative that was as popular. For most American viewers, it was just brilliant dog training coupled with the revolutionary claim that, with time, dedication, work, and listening to the dog's animal needs, even the most difficult case could be rehabilitated (as opposed to the available alternative, euthanasia). Audiences were transfixed by Millan's whispering techniques, by how quickly he could relax a dog or communicate with a dog and evoke the desired behavioral changes. And to many viewers who were already accustomed to the idea that dogs are naturally aggressive and dangerous and thus needed to be disciplined by being dominated, Millan introduced a revolutionary new perspective: that scary dog is actually just scared.

Today, we tend to forget how innovative the idea was for its time. Basic, crucial concepts like: (1) don't engage with a dog you are meeting for the first time (Millan's mantra "no talk, no touch, no eye contact") but let them come to you instead; (2) an aggressive dog is really an insecure dog; (3) entering into a training relationship is not about teaching this or that particular behavior, but about improving your bond and your dog's confidence; (4) dog training is more about humans than it is about dogs—it's the humans who must be taught how to live with dogs, not vice versa; (5) communication with dogs relies on energy and unspoken cues rather than words and commands—all of these continue to underpin "post-pack" positive reinforcement training today, when dominance-based training is definitely on the outs. Millan didn't invent these concepts but he did introduce them into mainstream culture.

He has also been a vocal advocate of the "pit bull"—a term

I'll use here in the way it's popularly used to refer to American pit bull terriers, American Staffordshire terriers, and more recently, all the pit mixes populating U.S. shelters. Millan's own celebrity dogs, first Daddy and later Junior, were American pit bull terriers, and their explicitly stated role on the show was to assist Millan in training by providing "calm assertive energy" to troubled dogs, teaching them dog manners and what Millan came to call "the pack code." But more than that, Millan's whole enterprise rests on the idea that there is no such thing as a dog that can't be rehabilitated, an idea to which the pit bull breeds pose the biggest challenge in the American public imagination. Contemporary breed bans do not distinguish between them, and, as Dayan explains, the American pit bull terrier as a breed is on its way out, with the most favored bloodlines being actively destroyed before our eyes.[1] The war on pit bulls, from housing bans to euthanasia automatically prescribed for any dog that's suspected to come from a fighting background, is a direct refutation of the beliefs of Millan and many other trainers that any dog can be rehabilitated with enough time, effort, and education. It begins with the founding assumption that aggression can be bred into and out of dogs, a belief that pit bull advocates are working hard to expose as false.

Thus, Millan's contributions to dog life and to training culture have been considerable, and much greater than his many critics like to admit. At the same time that he popularized ideas still espoused today, however, he also popularized the notion of the pack leader, which had in fact been discredited as a model of domestic dog behavior since at least the 1970s.

Millan's methods—no, his very existence—have given professional trainers something to talk about, if only to position

---

1. See chapter 5 of Dayan, *With Dogs at the Edge of Life*.

themselves against it. His approach could be called balanced training, because it uses a combination of corrections or aversive techniques and positive reinforcement. But even other fellow balanced trainers openly reject his approach, precisely because Millan is a dominance theory–based practitioner. While all trainers agree that owners must set boundaries in order for dogs to be happy and healthy—this is perhaps the most basic assumption underlining the need for training in the first place—Millan insists that the most basic expression of a boundary is that the dog is not the "leader." It is a framework that equates setting boundaries with correction and "consequences," another word for punishment, however broadly conceived.

These distinctions are important. Today's balanced training techniques don't rely on a pack-leader framework. And balanced training's newest competitor, called "pure positive," holds that no corrections should be used, only positive reinforcement. It has its own celebrity trainer, Victoria Stillwell, who had a multiseason show called *It's Me or the Dog*. Pure positive instills boundaries using a noncorrective method called boundary games. Though the approaches understand themselves to be in opposition, they agree on one important thing: owners can create boundaries without relying on an outdated concept of their own dominance or of trying to curtail their dog's imagined quest for dominance.

The notion of the pack as it is commonly understood today is grounded in "alpha theory," introduced by Swiss zoologist Rudolf Schenkel in 1947 in his landmark study "Expression Studies on Wolves." Based on his study of captive, unrelated wolves, Schenkel concluded that packs consist of individuals who fight for dominance, and such fights result in the strongest individual, the alpha, leading the pack. His findings—true, but only of captive, unrelated wolves—were erroneously extrapolated onto wild wolves and then onto dogs and finally dog–human interaction. By the time Barry Lopez published his gorgeous popular scientific work *Of Wolves and Men* in 1976, he was already referring to "alpha" as a term that "evolved to describe captive animals" and "is still misleading."[2]

Later wolf researchers, most notably David Mech, consistently confirmed that the alpha paradigm does not apply to wolves in the wild, who live in families and are led by breeding pairs, not individuals. The breeding pair mates for life and are the oldest individuals in the group, the ones who never leave. They are not "dominant" in any of the usual meanings—they are simply the parents. Furthermore, as Mech and others have shown, behaviors of dominance and submission appear among individuals on a regular basis—they are behaviors, not inherent character traits. And they have nothing to do with aggression or submission to aggression. They are healthy, normal negotiations of access to resources, in the service of a well-functioning family ensemble.[3]

Wolves are endlessly fascinating—so much so that no one seemed to notice that none of this had anything to do with dogs. Applied to dogs, the alpha idea is even less appropriate, and applied to humans—understanding themselves to be the alphas dominating their own dogs—it's just plain dangerous, some trainers argue. Almost half a century later, the shift has yet to happen in the popular imagination.

But this is only the tip of the iceberg when it comes to Millan's approach. Perhaps the most important reason Millan receives so much flak from other trainers is that his training is hard to describe as a unified vision at all. He appears to many trainers as internally inconsistent, giving owners a great deal of confusing information that, rather than empowering them, keeps

2. Lopez, 33.
3. David Mech, "Alpha Status, Dominance, and Division of Labor in Wolf Packs," *Canadian Journal of Zoology* 77: 1196–1203, http://www.npwrc.usgs.gov/resource/2000/alstat/alstat.htm.

them trapped in the "whisperer" fantasy that Millan possesses a unique gift. Indeed, when it comes to the training on *The Dog Whisperer,* there were a lot of mixed messages, ones for which trainers and savvy owners have been calling him out for years. Millan routinely appeared to dominate insubordinate large dogs with methods he continuously urged us not to try at home, from cornering a scared, reactive dog, to simulating a bite with his hand, jabbing his fingers into a dog to correct, to lightly kicking a dog in order to interrupt fixation, to grabbing a dog by the throat (like the mom would do, he always said) and pushing it down on the ground to "force submission." He used corrective collars and allowed for controversial use of them, such as picking a slip-collared dog up by the leash in order to completely immobilize it. The video that most of his detractors use to illustrate that Millan is clueless about what he is doing is the famous "Cesar Millan Hangs Shadow"[4] video. Millan kicks a husky while walking him, who then reacts by trying to bite Millan. What follows is a long and stomach-turning sequence in which Millan picks up the dog by its slip lead to curtail what he calls his "dominant" behavior, effectively hanging Shadow, who by now is showing signs of asphyxiation. Ultimately Millan "dominates" Shadow by forcing the choking, slightly spasmodic dog to the ground. Millan even points out Shadow's erection, while the dogs lies still on the ground, claiming that this is further proof of Shadow's dominant behavior, while his critics insist that the erection is actually a sign of asphyxiation.

The Dog Whisperer always began with a disclaimer—"do not try this at home"—but since it was all about empowering owners to defend their space, hold their ground, assert their authority over dogs that were not listening, it was hard to take the dis-

4. https://www.youtube.com/watch?v=Pw3glB4qQPY&t=94s.

claimer seriously. And while many of the lessons were active—and indeed, as Millan repeated over and over, dangerous to try without the assistance of a trainer—some of them were simply about what to stop doing. His favorite was to tell people to stop treating their dogs like children and indulging their tantrums. This was clearly a message not just to the show's guests, but to viewers as well.

Millan has on many occasions discouraged owners from doing something that many of us immediately do instinctively when we know our dogs are anxious or scared. We touch them, massage them to relax them, or pick them up off the ground, for their own safety or that of others. This, Millan claims, should be avoided because it simply encourages the dog's bad behavior. But this recommendation depends on a fundamental misunderstanding of how anxiety works, the kind of behavior it is. Fear or anxiety is not an operant or chosen behavior. It's a respondent behavior, immediate and unconscious, which means there is no such thing as either rewarding or punishing it. Or rather, regardless of how often I punish my dog for being afraid, it won't stop the next time she is afraid. In fact, calming down a fearful, reactive dog is a good idea, because the reactivity is less likely to continue to escalate. Many trainers argue for classically conditioning dogs in situations in which they are anxious by, precisely, rewarding them in the presence of the trigger. Comforting touch or a treat in that situation is not a "reward" in the true sense but an abrupt shift in feelings and associations from negative to positive. This is precisely how crate training works, for example. And Millan does plenty of classical conditioning on his show, as well.

Since so much of his product was based on the idea that dogs misbehave because they are anxious, Millan also routinely mischaracterized them as being relaxed when they were not, usually minutes into the training session, as proof that his methods worked. While classic markers of anxiety, such as panting, abound in every episode, Millan points to the dog and says look: he or she is finally relaxed, because we've set a boundary.

Much of Millan's advice is, as even he sometimes points out, counterintuitive. But in many cases, that's simply a sign that it's wrong. Still, my goal here is not to challenge Millan but rather to understand the hold his show has on the public. He continues to be the undisputed champion of mainstream TV about dogs. In 2020, National Geographic briefly revived *The Dog Whisperer* with an episode titled "The Year of the Dog"—an appropriate comment on the role that dogs played during the Covid lockdown. And in 2021 National Geographic premiered his new series, called *Better Human, Better Dog,* based on an introductory sequence that posits Covid for why the dog whisperer had to be reanimated: the shelters are empty, which means that more people than ever need help with their dogs.

On his TikTok channel, Millan even made an "Alors on Danse" TikTok,[5] participating in the massively popular trend in which a person sways gently to a clip of music while the text above them refers to something they feel massively triumphant about, usually in response to naysayers. Millan's reads "when your new show comes out on National Geographic today." And while his infectious smile indicates that the whole thing is light and a joke, there's no getting around how much criticism Millan receives on TikTok, so that this can easily be read as a response: haters gonna hate, but I'm back and I'm still the king.

Many people today continue to use the language of the pack, the alpha, and dominance—with little idea of what it means or how to use it correctly with respect to dogs. In every dog-problems or dog-behavior group I belong to on Facebook, I see people responding to posts about behavioral issues with "you've

5. https://www.tiktok.com/@imcesarmillan/video /6990781546575793414

got to make the rules! You're the alpha!" "Your chihuahua needs to know who's boss!" as well as rampant misuse of the concept of dominance and submission. Alpha theory may be over, but it continues to enjoy great success with audiences. What was—and what continues to be—the draw of this way of understanding dogs, and of shaping dog–human ensembles?

This is a different question from *What is the draw of Cesar Millan?*, a question we can ask about any celebrity, and which people have managed to answer only by gesturing toward mystique and the "it factor." But how much of the success of his enterprise is attributable to his "it factor" and how much to the appeal of the pack narrative? After all, the "pack code" is a term he invented and defined as "loyalty, honesty, and integrity," qualities that humans look for in their human-to-human relationships, and ones that are in particularly short supply in conditions of social scarcity and global precarity.

Millan has always been fond of saying, "I rehabilitate dogs, I train people." This was in fact one of his great contributions to owner culture, the idea that it is humans who are mishandling the relationship. But his training of people is equally confusing. While he explicitly asks owners to not treat their dogs like their children, because dogs are dogs, not people, he relies on the pack structure model for the dog–human ensemble, coaching humans to behave like actual dog moms.

What Is a Social Animal?

In Millan's shows, the true message to and about people is much bigger than the one he has for dog owners. The show itself—specifically, everything that culturally underlies the immediate directions to humans to do this or that—is a commentary on social life and social structure. And here lies the power of the concept of the wolf pack.

It's worth noting here that this is not the wolf pack of Deleuze and Guattari. In their classic work *A Thousand Plateaus: Capitalism and Schizophrenia,* the pack is of an entirely different nature than the family or the state. Animal packs are what "works" the family or the state "from within" and troubles them "from without," they write—the quintessential threat to everything that humans know as order. Deleuze and Guattari's pack does not reproduce—it is contagious, or rather, it is "nature" as contagion itself. "That is the only way Nature operates—against itself."[6] As I've argued elsewhere, sex can become figured as contagion (as it did in the case of Chernobyl and the ensuing imaginary of radiation passed down congenitally), especially in the context of wilderness and animality.[7] In that case, reproduction itself becomes unproductive, a form of contagion by the monstrous. In stark contrast to Deleuze and Guattari's pack, alpha theory is precisely the promise of family and state— except done well this time, because it is done by animals and not humans, and so in accord with nature.

Every Millan episode is not only about a particularly unruly dog but is also fueled by its human-interest story. The first episode of *Better Human, Better Dog,* for example, features two young, heterosexual couples who are having trouble moving on to the "next stage" of their relationships because of a problematic dog. The first couple plans to move in together but fears exposing the woman's young son to the man's fixated pit bull. The second

6. Gilles Deleuze and Félix Guattari, *A Thousand Plateaus: Capitalism and Schizophrenia*, trans. Brian Massumi (Minneapolis: University of Minnesota press, 1987), 242.

7. See Margret Grebowicz, "Ecology after Dark: Chernobyl's Wild Horses and the Traffic in Desire," *Minnesota Review* 96 (2021), https://read.dukeupress.edu/the-minnesota-review/article-abstract/2021/96/56/173390/Ecology-after-DarkChernobyl-s-Wild-Horses-and-the?redirectedFrom=fulltext.

couple are newlyweds who would like to have a baby but instead have an aggressive yorkie, who is also an Instagram and TikTok influencer. The episode ends with Millan teaching both men how to become better pack leaders, thus unifying these families into well-functioning reproductive units, including two heterosexual adults, children, and dogs—a very specific picture of what counts as a good pack living happily ever after.

But I suspect the appeal is becoming even more abstract than that. The fantasy of the pack begins with the basic assumption that we know what a successful social structure is supposed to look like at all. In other words, it's not particular stories that Millan's show tells of how to become better-functioning social beings, but the fantasy that such improvement is possible with the help of a handful of learnable, scientifically backed techniques. The appeal of the pack is its clarity and neatness as an idea, its easy communicability, and its apparently easy transferability from canine-only to canine–human ensembles. It's firmly rooted in a reality—that humans are animals—but one that leads to innumerable projections onto both human and nonhuman animals and to an imaginary in which social life is observable, understandable, predictable, and manageable—exactly as we imagine it to be for nonhuman animals. As much as Millan likes to repeat that interactions with dogs are emotional and not rational, the overarching desire behind a well-trained pack is a deep desire for living rationally. It's a feeling, but the feeling is a desire for rational, well-ordered, predictable, and thus manageable social organization.

Millan's own pack has boasted up to sixty-five dogs at a time, though now it's at around thirty.[8] Presumably because of his

8. Nina Metz, "'Dog Whisperer' Cesar Millan on Why American Have So Many Problems with Their Dogs," *Chicago Tribune*, February 16, 2017, https://www.chicagotribune.com/entertainment/tv/ct-cesar-millan-tv-chicago-0217-20170216-column.html.

wealth and expertise, no one worries that his packs may constitute hoarding. On the contrary, the show's introductions and endings are rife with exhilarating or slow-motion imagery of Millan running on a beach with multiple dogs running behind him, or walking what looks like ten dogs on lead, all of whom trot dutifully behind him, their leader. The show's guests come with their dyadic relationships—even when there is more than one dog in the family, Millan rightly asks that the person work with one dog, one problem at a time—but they enter a multidog, interspecies utopia. It is precisely the same utopia that fuels dog hoarding, considered animal abuse when practiced in low-income contexts. Millan is able to live like this thanks to his wealth and many hired hands, not thanks to his dog training experience.[9]

The biggest mistake we can make as critics of alpha theory is to assume that what appeals to humans is the aspect of dominance. What actually appeals is something much more difficult to challenge: the idea that social units—for example, families—make sense and can be understood and managed. More deep than an idea, at work is the *desire* that social units function this way. The persistent appeal of the pack has little to do with humans' desire to dominate dogs, but it has everything to do with humans' desire for something that seems ever further out of reach: a manageable life with each other.

9. For another version of this argument, see Margret Grebowicz, "You Are Not the Boss of Your Dog," *Slate,* September 21, 2021, https://slate.com/technology/2021/09/cesar-millan-dominance-theory-dog-training.html.

Conclusion: *Familiaris*

CANIS LUPUS FAMILIARIS, the domestic dog, is a subspecies of *Canis lupus,* the gray wolf. In other words, wolves and dogs are not distinct species.

What are we to make of this? What have we made of this? What will we make?

"Easy certainty undermines what matters most in the mutuality of adaptation between humans and dogs," Dayan writes.[1] She is speaking about mutual regard and openness, what she and Haraway both call "respect." For these two thinkers, dog–human relationships provide a delicious, murky uncertainty, the one that accompanies taking someone seriously as a subject with an inner life of their own: an other person. Without this, we have nothing. In her critique of Derrida in *When Species Meet,* Haraway faults Derrida for not being interested in the cat's inner life, not really. "He came right to the edge of respect," she writes, but "failed a simple obligation of companion species; he did not become curious about what the cat might actually be doing, feeling, thinking, or perhaps making available to him."[2]

1. Dayan, 21.
2. Haraway, 20.

Simple obligation of companion species, what matters most in the mutuality of adaptation—these are the guiding frameworks for thinking about dogs in recent years, ones that focus on intimacy, relation, reciprocity, and ethics. But today we are witnessing the emergence of a different paradigm for understanding the role of dogs in our lives, one grounded in the extreme vulnerability of our *social* selves. Dogs are no longer simply our best friends in the private, domestic sphere—or rather, what was once the private, domestic sphere is quickly becoming the stuff of public life, discourse, and politics, right down to an obsession with uncovering the truth about the history of domestication—for dogs and humans alike, as we confront our shared captivity and exclusion from the "state of nature." At stake is something other than ethics, or relations between individuals—it's the social itself in a better state, a healed state.

"What matters most" between dogs and humans is thus not a constant, or a fact that can be excavated in the course of evolutionary-biological or paleoanthropological discoveries and put on display in a museum of natural history. "What matters most" undergoes change as the nature of social life undergoes change. These changes are reflected in the changes in dog-owner culture.

We have known for a while that the desire for certainty in a relationship with another being is a sort of category mistake. And (at least) the past two decades of theory have taught us that it comes at a price: the foreclosure of possibility. But when we come to see that desire as part of a much broader extractive process, the error becomes more than epistemological—looking for certainty where none is possible—and even more than ethical—turning away from otherness, openness, or the generative power of "the open." It becomes an aesthetic or libidinal issue, verging on cathexis, a fixation that's not quite appropriate to the situation. And when it is reflected in and indeed shapes and even creates practices—in this case, the practices that make up dog ownership—it becomes real, creating the very material reality that is subject to the mutual adaptive process, down to the very chemistry of feelings. On all sides.

"Ah, but one is never useless to his dog," John Mclaughlin writes.[3] No wonder there are such experiences of intensity and meaning between people and dogs, as both species coevolve in direct response to the pressure of increasing meaninglessness, feelings of uselessness, and relational bankruptcy.

As owners, we are pushing each other and ourselves to "do better" in this form of relation, which for many of us is the relation par excellence, the ethical encounter stripped down to its essence. All of that may be true—and it is certainly true that we should do better—but it's important to realize and not forget that this demand unfolds not in a vacuum but under the pressure of social scarcity.

The goal, then, is not just to do better in these conditions but to do differently, to allow new paradigms to emerge from life with dogs. To let our dogs help us to change.

"Now let's go further," Dayan writes. She invites us to think again about dogs, but in ways that don't project from the human onto the dog. The arrow of projection should actually be reversed, she argues correctly. The neuroscience imposing human measurement frameworks and analytical tools onto dog minds has it exactly backwards: it's dogs that actually provide "the ground for human sensibility and cognition"—or rather, it's this extraordinary, primeval, intimately co-adaptive relationship, without which neither dogs nor humans would be what they are. Borrowing once more from Anna Lowenhaupt Tsing, I would name this phenomenon an assemblage, a unit whose "elements

3. McLaughlin, x.

are contaminated and thus unstable; they refuse to scale up smoothly."[4] She also calls assemblages "scenes for considering livability—the possibility of common life on a human-disturbed earth," which is precisely how I am trying to frame the dyad.[5]

I sometimes wonder if such reimagining could answer the hunger humans seem to have for the wolf pack. Deleuze and Guattari's fascination with the wolf pack is itself contagious, and dreamy. But it relies on a willful forgetting of the individual, when in fact, the extraordinary social capacities of wolves are what allows for the development of strongly differentiated, individual personalities. It is the very stability of social organization and the effectiveness of communication that allows individual temperaments to mature in pack societies.[6] A wolf pack "works" because of the sometimes dramatic differences among its individual members, not according to the logic of some undifferentiated, undulating, interconnected mass, or Deleuze and Guattari's other favorite, the swarm. It might be time to revisit the wolf pack as an imaginary—but to get it more right this time. "In such a terrain, even the word 'love' can be redeemed. And, perhaps, even the notion of 'human.'"[7] *Love* and *human*—both words that, to Dayan, are at present merely a shiny veneer on what is actually erasure, violence, and killing.

If we are indeed to do better and go further, what is at stake from here on out is this terrain, the dog-human posthuman. We can no longer afford to forget that this terrain is coextensive with the late capitalist social imaginary. No, even that phrase

4. Tsing, 43.
5. Tsing, 163.
6. Lopez, 18.
7. Colin Dayan, "Dogs Are Not People," *Boston Review,* January 12, 2014, https://bostonreview.net/books-ideas/colin-dayan-dogs-are-not-people-humanity.

doesn't get at the heart of it: more than an imaginary, it's the most powerful and all-pervasive affective milieu in which we live, that of the very *vitality* that is living with others and living in an environment. And a large part of its power today comes from the fact that this vitality suffers from seemingly continuous and bottomless attrition, like a descending Shepard tone.

Dog abundance and proximity doesn't always have nice effects. The assemblage isn't soft and fuzzy. A study has just been announced that shows that hookworms have evolved a resistance to all of the drugs we currently have to kill them. This has happened because in greyhound racing kennels, the dogs were so susceptible to catching hookworms from each other that they were treated for them more often than would normally be called for. The resistant worms survived the treatments, and researchers predict that they will now spread to dogs outside of racing kennels. As retired racing greyhounds are adopted into homes, the worms will be passed on to other dogs, and as dogs meet other dogs in dog parks, the infection will spread. And hookworms can be passed from dogs to humans—which was not the end of the world, as long as we had drugs to fight them.[8]

Can dogs rescue humans from the coming end of the social—whether real or imagined? I believe they can—that perhaps only *they* can. But it won't be recognizable as a rescue operation. It will require some changes in perspective on the part of humans first. Calling for respect for and openness to the other is no longer enough. Creating and adopting more and more dogs is not enough, if this does nothing to destabilize the machines of dispossession that govern our world. Even calling for more and better technologies of the essential self is not enough,

8. Leigh Beeson, "Dog Parasite Is Developing Resistance to Treatments," *UGA Today,* September 21, 2021, https://news.uga.edu /hookworms-are-developing-resistance-to-medications/.

if we don't also recognize that the essence of the self is embeddedness and relationships.

Dogs have always been humans' partners in survival, and I believe they can help us survive even the unlivable present. But this requires basic changes in infrastructure to reflect that we are ready, for the first time in human history, to own up to and prioritize our relationship with and dependency on a nonhuman animal. As long as humans are not ready to receive the help, we cannot be helped.

Can we make better relationships under the relentless pressure of social scarcity, in order to find our way out of it? Can we see the dog-human posthuman for what it really is, even as we, imagining ourselves as the intelligent observers capable of taking stock of the situation, grapple at every moment with a crisis of affect, the affective crisis that is slow death? Can we create dog-human practices that actually allow for new forms of sociality to emerge, ones we have not yet seen? With these questions—and with the concrete practical changes they imply—we are in the strange position of beholding this ancient, original posthuman assemblage as if we were seeing it for the first time.

And yet, none of this is new. The ancient Egyptian god Anubis, who guards the entrance to the underworld, is half wolf, half man—in most depictions. In some, however, he is simply an African wolf, sleek, muscular, shiny black, with narrow, almond eyes and tall, sharp ears.[9] It's commonplace to describe him as the god of the dead, as if he simply watched over dead people. In fact, Anubis is the ultimate judge of the living. He not only guards the gates of the afterlife, he attends the scales on which

9. For years, Anubis was thought to be an Egyptian jackal, which recent DNA evidence has identified as an African wolf.

the human heart is weighed prior to allowing the soul to enter. Don't be fooled by the stylized, ornate imagery. In the end, it's a wild dog that judges the human heart.

Out there, right at the edges of our collective late-capitalist captivity, is the wilderness, their wilderness. My own dogs know that wilderness doesn't belong to them. When I walk them at dusk, they become anxious and impatient to return home. For domestic dogs, dusk means imminent danger. For wild canids, it means the party has just begun.

One early cool, fall evening recently, I was picking mushrooms in the forest and suddenly was awash in an exquisite vocal cacophony. Coyotes. They weren't nearby, and I'm sure they weren't interested in me, but they were unmistakably communicating to each other across the forest through which I happened to be traipsing. I wasn't exactly scared for myself, but I was secretly relieved that, this one time, Abba wasn't with me, that I didn't have to fear for her, since coyotes sometimes kill dogs. (I am always very aware of this fact when Waffles wakes me up to go out at night, his little chihuahua body the perfect size of a coyote supper.)

It's funny that my first instinct is to fear for my dogs, when historically it was dogs that have killed wolves in wolf hunts as well as on farms, where dogs were traditionally protection against coyotes and foxes. Irish wolfhounds, the largest dogs in the world, came into existence for this very reason, to kill wolves. But my dogs seem like a whole other species from those true working dogs of old, and they stand no chance against a pack of coyotes. And coyotes are here, everywhere. Wolves are far away, in cold, brutal, spectacular national parks and protected wilderness areas, but coyotes are everywhere that humans are. Right around the bend. I never see them, but their songs—what songs!—are an unmistakable reminder that humans and canids, both wild and domestic, continue to coevolve, even now, when it feels like "everything that is to be done is as if it were already done."[10]

This year there are more coyotes than usual, or maybe it's just that they are coming closer than usual. It's been an exceptionally wet summer, and that probably has all sort of effects on their ecosystem that I don't even begin to understand. All I know is that it's fall, and every day at dusk, when that exquisite chill creeps across the field and the sky is still pink, they howl over the hill up the road from my house. Sometimes they howl down the hill. Often they wake me up when it's still dark with their howling, out there, moving freely, a pack of wild things, while my dogs snuggle even more tightly under the covers, unmistakably afraid. I am their family, not the coyotes outside. Sometimes we go to listen in the doorway. Close together, safely inside and framed by a sliding glass door, we behold the inky darkness from which they call out. They know we are here, and they certainly know we can hear them. I fantasize that they can even see our silhouettes framed by the tall rectangle of light.

What do my dogs feel when they hear coyotes? Are they encountering creatures like themselves or something else, someone alien? Helen Mort writes about her dogs chasing a badger, whom they can never catch not only because he happens to outrun them but for a more mysterious reason: "The badger belongs to a world they can't reach, as private and inaccessible as their world is to me."[11] But we know that the distance between wild and domestic dogs is not nearly as great. On the evolutionary scale, it's almost nothing. Who are domestic dogs in the ongoing dance between

10. Jean-François Lyotard, *Postmodern Fables,* trans. Georges Van Den Abbeele (Minneapolis: University of Minnesota Press, 2000), 8.
    11. Mort, 91.

wild canids and humans, in which humans must protect their dogs from wolves, coyotes, and even foxes, the very same animals who simultaneously thrive in more or less hidden proximity to humans? As domestic dogs become our family members, are wild dogs our not-yet-domesticated companions, as sort of dog of the future, coming ever closer, more and more dependent on patterns of human life, patterns that depend on so strongly on the life force that is *Canis?*

One thing is for sure: they're watching.

(Continued from page iii)

Forerunners: Ideas First

Nicholas Tampio
Learning versus the Common Core

Kathryn Yusoff
A Billion Black Anthropocenes or None

Kenneth J. Saltman
The Swindle of Innovative Educational Finance

Ginger Nolan
The Neocolonialism of the Global Village

Joanna Zylinska
The End of Man: A Feminist Counterapocalypse

Robert Rosenberger
Callous Objects: Designs against the Homeless

William E. Connolly
Aspirational Fascism: The Struggle for Multifaceted Democracy under Trumpism

Chuck Rybak
UW Struggle: When a State Attacks Its University

Clare Birchall
Shareveillance: The Dangers of Openly Sharing and Covertly Collecting Data

la paperson
A Third University Is Possible

Kelly Oliver
Carceral Humanitarianism: Logics of Refugee Detention

P. David Marshall
The Celebrity Persona Pandemic

Davide Panagia
Ten Theses for an Aesthetics of Politics

David Golumbia
The Politics of Bitcoin: Software as Right-Wing Extremism

Sohail Daulatzai
Fifty Years of *The Battle of Algiers*: Past as Prologue

Gary Hall
The Uberfication of the University

Mark Jarzombek
Digital Stockholm Syndrome in the Post-Ontological Age

N. Adriana Knouf
How Noise Matters to Finance

Andrew Culp
Dark Deleuze

Akira Mizuta Lippit
**Cinema without Reflection: Jacques Derrida's Echopoiesis
and Narcissism Adrift**

Sharon Sliwinski
Mandela's Dark Years: A Political Theory of Dreaming

Grant Farred
Martin Heidegger Saved My Life

Ian Bogost
The Geek's Chihuahua: Living with Apple

Shannon Mattern
Deep Mapping the Media City

Steven Shaviro
No Speed Limit: Three Essays on Accelerationism

Jussi Parikka
The Anthrobscene

Reinhold Martin
Mediators: Aesthetics, Politics, and the City

John Hartigan Jr.
Aesop's Anthropology: A Multispecies Approach

Margret Grebowicz is associate professor of humanities at University of Silesia in Katowice, Poland. Her most recent books include *The National Park to Come, Whale Song,* and *Mountains and Desire: Climbing vs. the End of the World.* She is the founding editor of the book series Practices, published by Duke University Press.